SWIM LESSONS

Poems

Maud Lavin

Tulipwood Books

Tulipwood Books | Mercer Island, WA
tulipwood.org

Published 2025 by Tulipwood Books
Printed in the United States of America

Edited by Lynne Ellis
Book and Cover Design by Lynne Ellis and AJ Dent
Cover Art: *Agila Looking for Land #12* by Lucia Enriquez

First Edition

ISBN: 979-8-9914048-2-2

Library of Congress Control Number: 2025942009

Tulipwood Books is located on the unceded lands of the Duwamish, Muckleshoot, Cayuse, Umatilla, and Walla Walla people—past and present—who have cared for this land since time immemorial. These people are are still here, continuing to honor and bring light to this heritage, and we have great gratitude for their work.

Find out more at native-land.ca and duwamishtribe.org

Tulipwood Books

POETS & POEMS IN COLLABORATION

Contents

The Lake

The Flows

SWIM LESSONS

Introduction

Water is generous. It chops, soothes, slaps, embraces, buoys, sinks, laps, licks, comforts, repeats. It's erotic. Dangerous.

I love Lake Michigan. Love, love it. It's an inland sea, Michigan Ocean, freshwater life. My body hums near it, soothes in it, feels exhilarated. Even standing on the shore and looking out at the unbroken horizon will lift me. The Lake has 1638 miles of coast, much of it beach-lined, and each beach is home to those who splash, walk, mix there. 57th Street Beach in Chicago's Hyde Park is my home on the Lake—home for many on the South Side.

Swim Lessons starts with the Lake and moves to other flows, cutting a path through them, playing with connections of swimming and viewing, raising feelings of comfort and mortality, immersion and distance.

Thank you for traveling with me.

The Lake

Hanging Out

Sitting at the beach, now, staring at Lake Michigan.
Wading in the Lake's cold water, then back to sitting.
People watching at this Chicago beach,
checking out the swimming combos that aren't bathing suits—
cut-offs and T-shirts, short shorts and a sports bra.

God, I love to be bored. Teasing boredom. Hanging out.
Driving up and down Cleveland Avenue, stopping at Burger King.
Walking around that Ohio mall. And again.
Trying on lipstick samples till we're chased away.

My close-held hush—I grew up in the Midwest,
right in its small-town small heart, its expansive cornfields,
    its long, green summers.
It taught me to love hanging out. To blow up boredom like
    a balloon.

Dad and Son
at 57th Street Beach

Early in the season, a boy is dressed in his red bathing shorts
and blue inflated life jacket. He rides his orange bike to the beach,
    like a man's
bike with training wheels, he peddles next to his dad who walks,
    wearing his
cantaloupe-colored T-shirt, white shorts. The inflatable puffs out
    the boy's chest,
his father has his own puff, a middle-age tire, its comfortable
    curve,
respectable, earned by sitting at a desk somewhere during
    the week.
Their dark hair in matching haircuts, Dad with a beard and
    glasses.

The boy rides his bike across the large, sandy beach, not easy,
    right up to
the water's edge, hops off. His dad has left his sandals up close
    to the field house,
with their towels, and jogged to catch up. Not a lot of people
around, water still cold, but Dad and son are used to it. They know
the sandy shelf stretches far into the Lake here. They go for a
    water walk,

till the water is mid-thigh for the boy, mid-calf for Dad. They're
  talking,
striding along, arms and hands moving with the words, backs
  straight.
No wobbling in the sand, they stand tall, as always.
Dad and son couldn't care less who's watching, but still don't give
  an inch.
The water is steel today with highlights of blue, the clouds
  dipped in gray
underneath with fluffy white on top, expanding toward the
  horizon,
where they break and brighten. The Lake breathes with hope.
The boy makes a point, emphasizes with his left arm, Dad listens.

Recipe for Self-Care

Self-care does not have to be done alone.
You could, say, ride with your partner down
DuSable Lake Shore Drive in Chicago,
glimpsing the surprise aquamarine of the Lake.

Find free parking in Hyde Park, walk together
to 57th Street Beach, get bowled over by the view
as you approach, the reach of the shore and the trees.

Plant yourselves on the beach. Soak the sun.
Meet two actual mermaids, ages approximately seven and ten.
Sure, they look like little girls sticking their legs out together
while their friends cover the leg-tails with sand.
They say they are mermaids. Believe them.

Swim. Swim breaststroke in the chop of Lake Michigan.
Flip, stroke back, parallel to the beach, stand on the sandy shelf.
Dive in again and breaststroke the other way, lose count, flip,
stroke into the waves, get an earful, keep going, flip,
keep going, swim, swim, swim, wear a hat and sunglasses.

Go back to your love on the towels, say hi to the little mermaids,
flop down, body ironed out. Sink into the sand, buoyant.
Stare at the blue. The wispy clouds take you floating.

Forever Water

1

Oval Beach, Saugatuck, is a giant's open embrace. Its arms stretch the long arc of public beach as it blends into private, then public again, as far as the horizon. Its indent is a long, sandy shelf keeping swimmers and splashers safe. I wade way out to swim, plunge into breaststroke, frog kick, as if I could go forever. We've traveled three hours to get here, to indulge in the Lake and blueberry muffins, freshwater, fresh blueberries. Later, back home in Chicago, I read about forever chemicals in freshwater fish. I want to refuse to believe. I go to 57th Street Beach, another safe unroll of a sandy shelf. More wading to swim, little kids stay shallow, older gents with arm muscles and pot bellies swim further out, and me with them. I feel the water as clean, though I know it's not.

2

I remember a decade ago, swimming in Lake Superior, the cleanest water I've ever seen, forever seen, clear to the bottom of that gigantic Great Lake. So pure. Forever chemicals there, too. Forever water, my water, our water, freshwater.

3

Ungleichzeitigkeit—German—the state of not being at the same time, nonsynchronous. Oh, but Ernst Bloch took that clumsy word to some heights in his Marxist, utopian, loopy, inspiring, antifascist writing. Tormented in Weimar Germany by the rising popularity of the Nazis, he saw their followers looking back to blood-and-soil myths to look forward to dreams of the Third Reich, and asked how else, how else could we look back to look forward? What about those *Spuren*, those traces, those moments, that meant so much to us in the past, can they provide a chute into a better, more just future, a more sharing and caring one? This is a question I hold to my heart, a century after he so urgently asked it.

4

I close my eyes and daydream the water in Center Lake, Stark County, Ohio, water we knew was clean, and how swimming there as kids made us happy, and the well water we drank, and the marshes we waded, in springtime, when the ground started to give again and crunch hard then soft as we soaked our shoes and walked across, and the Water Hole, where we watched the small lake down the street empty its water underneath the unpaved road into the small pond and then the pond into the marsh. We were landlocked, we were surrounded by water we loved.

5

I bring all that in my body every time I wade, then plunge into Lake Michigan. Every time I read of threats to its water I want to protect it, and more I want to embrace it and be embraced by it. I'll never let go of this imperfect inland sea, never stop feeling grateful. My beauty.

57ᵗʰ Street Beach

Capture, release, capture, release,
I take photos of the clean, sandy expanse,
enjoy the company: people of many races and ages.
We're a postcard for Chicago: *God Bless
the Chicago Park District.* I remember when
this beach was grungy, my toddler niece cut her foot
on some glass. Now it's clean, raked, sifted, sand-filled,
day after day, summer after summer, I worship
this beach. I love walking on the sand:
its smooth heat, its cool comfort,
the long welcoming shelf under the water.
The lifeguards bob in rowboats, keeping a close
eye. Kids play in the water, so many kids, so many
different colors. Families watch, join. This is what
government should do. Keep up the beaches
and the parks, keep the schools safe, fix the potholes,
support the unions, fix the bridges. This is what
the government should not do: terrorize us.

Meanwhile the Chicago Park District carries on, beautifully.

And I photograph—one puff cloud drifts down, kids play
in an accidental V, the horizon is impossibly far in this Great
Lake, Promontory Park peeks from the left, and I

tuck my phone in my purse, leave my purse with my husband,
walk the sand, enter the cold, safe water, amble and wade in
  the water,
toward the dangerous deep but staying embraced in the lifeguard
  territory,
with the families, with my reading husband taking a glance.
And I release and plunge, cold!

I breaststroke parallel to the shore, wonder about how
  photography
is like and unlike swimming, then I don't care, I feel nothing
but stroke, kick, glide, move, swim, water, water, water, air.

Imaginary Friends

It's September, the air is warm, the Lake has started to cool,
the Park beaches are closed throughout Chicago.
No lifeguards, swimmers beware. Red flag up.
Waves high and choppy. Sky clear cerulean blue.

Hardly anyone in the water. What to do?
Ah, a woman about my age, white one-piece,
low cut in back, she's going in. Doing fine.
Thinner than I am. Still I count her as kin.

I get up and walk into the water, feel the chop,
safe though, both feet on the sandy shelf, go
deeper, more, water up to mid-chest, feel
the waves. Not sure about plunging.

She's already walking back. Oh!, her tummy is
a bit poochie like mine. Sister. It's good to see
people of all ages at this beach, all body types,
including mine, including hers. I look for the older
women at the beach—my imaginary friends.
I stand, waves hitting, thump, smack, think of diving.
Instead, stay chest deep, stroll on the shelf.

Now she's real shallow, doing half push-ups
in the water. Yes, good idea. Mainly just
lolling around. Me, too. I stroll back
along the shelf to the beach, splash, rock.

My legs feel great. Back on the towel.
I spot another woman my age. With her grown daughter?
The older woman also wears a low-cut swimsuit
and an orange, sleeveless, wrap blouse.

I see you, gracefully draping that belly,
without shame, or so I imagine, with more
of a this-is-my-business stride. Looking
good, standing tall, walking the shore
on the sand, straw visor on, getting steps in.
Do you know how much I love you?

Page of Cups

The heart of the matter, playfulness,
comfort and consolation in times of trouble,
water element symbolized by the Cup,
an impulse, an opportunity—the Page.

Crossed with the Empress. *Fertility,*
Growth, Creativity. She rules.
The question I asked
the Tarot cards: what is water?
What is water and swimming?

I do Tarot for others, have for decades,
since getting into it at Enchantments in the East Village,
the shop run by an actual coven.
Their magic candles, done in response to a request and
a consultation, like make-believe therapy, covered
with runes, essential oils like rose for love, glitter.
Instructions on making a positive visualization with
every lighting. Also on not burning your apartment down.

Full, rich, soothing, banana-pudding cards.
There are Cups all over this reading.
Ace of Cups in the place of the asker's emotions,
Nine of Cups for the near future.

Inexplicably, the far future reads the Five of Swords.
Discord, conflict, I'm worried.
How could the Lake give me that?
Will I lose the strength to swim? *Not yet,*
not yet.

I can't accept discord as the final word. I pull an extra card,
cross the Swords with the Eight of Pentacles—slow
apprenticeship and growth. Ah, ok, if my body gives out,
as it surely will, I can still build it back up
to swim again, to stroke, to glide, to breathe.

Spell

I step into the Lake, cold
takes me in, dull ankle pain
disappears, get beyond
invasive species shells,
Quagga mussels, to clear
sand, walk out deeper
my left knee rocks, meniscus
soreness disappears, shock
of cool water lapping my
labia tingles, I rise on my
toes, settle back into the sand,
keep going, in up to my waist,
my hips loosen, I splash
my arms, so does the Lake
water, now shivers, a wave
grasps my chest, laughs.
Oh!, stroke, breaststroke
breathe, frog kick, stroke, kick,
my back seizes then lets go,
stroke kick stroke kick mouthful spit
stroke kick, turn around, stroke kick,
view the shore, the horizon, the blue sky.
The water lifts me. High.

My Dream, My Love,
the City on the Lake

The water plume in Buckingham Fountain parachutes up.
Next to it, a Victorian balloon ride, a flame
inside the balloon keeping it afloat.
A door swings open in the giant straw basket,
I climb in, the sandbags drop, and we lift off.

We hold at forty feet up, still tethered to the earth.
Looking south, I see the head and raised arms of the Golden Lady,
a replica towering over the green trees of Hyde Park.
East, south, north, the Lake, aqua, huge, not a crease, holding its breath.

The Lake in My Living Room

A gift from Jin Lee,
photographer,
friend,
fellow Lake lover,
fellow swimmer,
this photo of Lake Michigan could only be taken by her.
A gift for the eye.
The horizon is un-tilted,
whether from the capturing or the printing,
looks completely horizontal,
you could swim a leveler on it.
The clouds are continuous,
balanced with blue sky,
the light diffused,
muted touches of gorgeous pink reflected.
Then the slightest touches of pink surface on the dark blue,
undulating water.
The intense look,
the components of beauty bared.
In this photo,
the Lake neither invites nor pushes away,
it appears.
It has its own existence;
this image is for the eyes only.
The accumulation of much looking and reflecting.
The generous understanding and sharing of beauty.
Thank you, Jin.

Craters

Start in Sheboygan, Wisconsin.
Yes, that Sheboygan.
Get in a boat, go
about fourteen miles southeast.
Look into the water
about five hundred feet, that's fifty stories of a building.
You might need sonar.
Zigzag south toward Port Washington.
Keep looking.
Find forty round craters in the seabed.

Do they mark the remains of an ancient civilization?
The lairs of deep-sea monsters?
Swimming pools for mermaids?
Maybe mermaids don't always want to swim with fish.

I want to believe in ancient civilizations,
ones more technological,
more just, more fair—
succeeding where we've failed.
But weak too—unable to survive.
If there were ancient civilizations
and they blew it, then when we blow it,
a few humans can rebuild in glory, deep in the sea.

One report says the craters are perfect circles,
but I can see in the photos that they're not,
and scientist after shipwreck hunter after scientist attest
they're not man-made. Still, I want them to be.
Maybe they're sinkholes created by water upwelling
through the limestone ground.
Or craters, or *splodges*—
as one observer says to belittle them.
They're huge, twenty to forty feet deep,
hundreds of feet in diameter.
Devoid of oxygen,
yet some have Quagga mussels.
And the bacteria they contain may be
akin to the earliest life-forms on Earth.
So: some evidence of an ancient civilization.
Not the kind that gives hope
for us to reinvent again and better, as long ago.
Instead, it's bacteria,
busy without us.

Being Held

The ferocious, beautiful
Lake is also a hugger, across
22,300 square feet of surface,
in the water below.
When it's gentle, when
I'm in the water near
the shore, its waves
push at me, my gyroscope
rights me, I lean
restfully into the water's
motion, it laps me, my skin's
surfaces, embracing me, I push
against it, and repeat, and
stroke, and am stroked.
What is swimming
if not trading
caresses. And ease.

Liquid Psalm to a Great Lake

Buoy my joints, float my limbs,
blur my hair, soothe my face,
hold me near, sing to me.
Living water embrace me, take
the stiffness from my spine, from my knees,
the weight from my shoulders, lift
my breasts, stay, stay, stay.
Move me along, scare me some,
feel my arms stroke your surface,
love me, push me, still me. Don't let me go.
I don't want to leave the Lake, don't want the burning land.
I stay afloat, I stay moving.
Keep me smooth, keep me safe.

When the What Ifs Turn into Nows

What if I stayed up as late as I wanted to every night
and slept in as late as I wanted to each morning.
What if I wrote an eco-novel with more mermaids
and jokes than pollution data and activism.
What if I dressed up in reds head to toe, the next day
maroons and my flowered velvet pants, to go to the café.
What if I invited all the Midwest writers I like from northern Wisconsin
to southern Ohio to read at my Chicago READINGS series.
And then with some of them, well, we become pals.
With others, I just wave them on their way, Midwestern nice.
I hear all of them, and sometimes read my own work, too.
What if I refuse to use the phone: texts and emails only.
What if I only hang out where I'm part of an easy diversity—
Jazz Showcase, Printers Row Wine Bar, 57th Street beach—
because it feels better and my whole body relaxes.
What if I swim in Lake Michigan, worship the Lake, make love
to the Lake, stroke the Lake, splash the Lake, duck my head under.
What if I'm unafraid to tell people how much I love their writing,
when I love their writing, and I enjoy reading them.
What if I tell Bruce how much I love him and what a slut he is,
every day—he is that beautiful, inside and out.
What if I keep in touch with my old friends,

my hometown neighbor since I was five and she was six,
my boyfriend in second grade,
the twins I hung out with in high school.
What if I decide to forgive my Ohio hometown and embrace it,
even while it shrinks back into the cornfields.
What if I keep and make friends of different ages,
because life is more interesting that way.
What if I love to write, so I do, and edit a little on the side.
What if I go to readings around town, listening and reading
my own work, shy, but feel glorious while performing.
What if I wear a mask at gallery openings, daring to be uncool.
What if I leave my hair gray, undercut, and weird.
What if I eat my sliced fruit with cocoa powder on it,
and get it everywhere. And am cocoa-scented.
What if I have way less money, but zero faculty meetings to attend.
What if I sleep better at night, and more,
and read more mysteries. What if I go for a walk each day,
using my walking sticks. What if I'm old and I use that
to know life is friable and devote mine to love, Lake Michigan,
cocoa powder, friendship, laziness, writing, readings.
What if you come visit Chicago, read at my READINGS series
         at the wine bar,
dress up any way you feel like, and have a latte with me after
         at the café?

The Flows

Topology

In mathematics, topology is *concerned with the properties of a geometric object that are preserved under continuous deformations, such as stretching, twisting, crumpling, and bending: that is, without closing holes, opening holes, tearing, gluing, or passing through itself.*

—from Wikipedia

The surfaces are constantly rolling and turning, and, on one surface, an abstracted figure twists and pulses with the movement. Apply a function to that figure, a function that stretches it and moves it to moan, well, in your mind it moans, here on paper there's no sound but there are steps, steps you make up. You apply another function, a different one. Do this on a Sunday afternoon early in your college years, lying on your bed, eating M&Ms, and using mathematical symbols, when it's summer and the windows are open. You love every minute of it. It feels like flying.

Only much later do you realize the safety inherent in this feral game—the figure holds, even while it transforms, it still exists. Everything changes it, but still it lasts. And the functions you invent are under your control even as they cause the figure to writhe and toss with the moving surfaces. Somehow, in ways you still don't understand, you can embrace this in your mind, like swimming, like the water embraces you when you swim.

By you, as you know, I mean me, but I use second person because it could be something that you could imagine too, if you were so inclined. It's made up but describable to a T, and so it can be shared, even transformed further, like a story. I did share such things, in fact, either in the theoretical math class I was taking or the one I was TAing. Really, I was teaching that one because when the instructor figured out I, the TA, liked not just to grade papers but to teach, and, well, it was summer, and he wanted to be outside, he often turned the class over to me. The students were premed, generally a year or two older than I was. I must've been about eighteen then. They didn't want to play as much as get a good grade and get into med school. I understood, but I taught them a bit about playing with mathematics anyway.

It was so beautiful, that play, like birds winging it in a gusty sky. Like lying on my back in a creek's current and being pulled along, watching the clouds, then closing my eyes and still knowing where I was going.

Night Walking

In Singapore, I exit the subway, alone,
after eleven at night, transfer
to the bus, wait in line at the stop,
grab a seat next to an unknown
man, stay on for four stops, climb off,
street dark, walk alone.

The air thick around me, also
soft and active like a runny egg.
I sweat, even this late at night—
the only one on the long ped-crossing
over the highway—I climb down the steps,
in front of a school, now dim except
for a security light or two. I see
the high-rises up ahead but no one
on this side of the street. Vegetation glints
in the night, tropically large, thick, scented. Sounds
I can't identify, animal, wind, coming from the density.

Yet, I feel so safe. I walk and glide, wrapped in the soft air,
thinking, in the equatorial night, of swimming tomorrow.

My love Chicago, not so safe.
Are those gunshots we hear, south aways?

We're going to Jazz Showcase,
three blocks north from our house.
Walking out together, my husband and me.
Maybe thirty degrees out, 7:30, winter dark.
Holiday lights, strings of them,
still on trees, around the yards, not a
cloud, the lights bright, glitter and shine.
Crisp air, crisp lights. Haven't been for a night walk
in ages. Here, I stroll alone only during the day.

As we walk, I remember Singapore, the unrelenting heat,
the generous nights, when I went around the city alone, sweating as if
bathing, unafraid. How welcoming: a city without threat, without guns.
A city that hugged me in the dark.

Clumsy Poem

I walk with walking sticks now. Spine damage.

Always clumsy, now I'm clumsier.

I give you my poetry as clumsy, too, at first with

long ungainly adverbs instead of blunt Anglo-Saxonisms.

Try to carry one, let's say, a romance language-rooted word,

blurry with syllables,

into a room sideways, under one arm, one walking stick in the
other hand,

only to have the word hit the door frame, and me to be pushed
back a step.

I draw back from neat language, like Wordle's—check, crisp,
waist, snort—

and words like my mother trying to assimilate, ones that aren't
Anglo-Saxon

but weigh like them—judge, repugnant, respectable, force.

I choose to be a tongue mutt, mixing long words like
romantically with

key short words like fresh, cute, straight, queer, bi—

a tongue explorer, who bounces back a step

and then walks into a room, stick first, tongue second,

holding ungraceful and taut, together.

Pivot

When I edit other people's writing, I try to hear how they're speaking to their imaginary friends.
Reaching, feeling how others might listen to and read the shared words.

When I write, I try to connect. I hold up my right hand, palm cupped in front of my face. It reminds me to talk to myself, to go some places that are playful, others that maybe I don't even want to go to.

Then the pivot, the glorious, sensual pivot, as I turn my wrist and face my palm outward, stretching out my arm. That pivot is hopping out, reaching for connection with others, thinking about how to touch them.

The writing needs to come in a size, and at a pitch, to travel to other ears already assaulted by busy sounds. Then, I let go. Because it won't travel as I want it to, or necessarily to the person I'm thinking of, or as soon as I want it to. But it travels.

Wrapping pieces for, reaching out to, others: to speak, to listen, to be heard, to hear. To touch and to be touched. To having control, and then letting it go.

Flying

I decided to take up flying fairly late in life. Had no idea what it entails. The good news first. Soaring! It's the best. Like the crows, you catch updrafts, you spread your arms, and soar upwards, hit different currents, clear skies, or foggy little clouds leaving drops of mist on your face. Then when you've gone high enough, so easy to inflate your parachute pants and let yourself drift downwards. Gently. The bad news? Well, flying requires more equipment than I'd thought. There's a lot of particulate pollution in the atmosphere, so you'd be well-advised to wear your N95 and goggles. Your instinct is to take great big gulps of air while flying, and you have to protect your eyes and lungs from those specks, deadly in cumulative amounts. There's the special parachute pants. And us permanent beginners need inflatables on our arms, too. Still, nothing can take away from the swoops and soars and floats and glides once you're up there. You go high enough, you can even see cool, calm Canada.

Bad Air Pumps Into the Plane

First rule of asthma attacks, remove
yourself from the area of irritation,
step outside a room filling with smoke,
walk away from that heavy perfume,
get away from the trigger.

Nowhere to go on a plane. So much fear.
I can't breathe, feel like I'm drowning. Trapped.
Emergency inhaler out. Shake it, prime it.
Inhale. It's not like on TV or movies
where the weak character, you know, the
one with asthma, takes a puff, or two,
looks ridiculous, but then can breathe.

No, the choking goes on. I cough up watery mucus.
I have to spit—into the paper towel, grabbed from my purse.
I look ridiculous. Also like I can't breathe.
My heart is racing. Fear and steroids.
Now I can breathe, but
I am still spitting up, blowing my nose.
My system has gone overboard.

I can't leave. So, I keep making a mess.
Breathing. Breathing. Coughing. Breathing.
I'm trying to breathe. I'm focusing on breathing.
And breathing. And breathing. Breathing.

Hi, 50ᵗʰ Reunion Yearbook

Hi, all, I hope you're doing really well and are Not Dead Yet, and if you are dead that you got cremated and were able to float in the wind, not end up in your loved one's face to be spit out and then land on their clothes, but instead could briefly fly and then swim in that body of water you'd picked for your final bob, and sink in the mud to be nosed at by a fish, and then left to rest in peace. Love, Maud

Bodies, Water

Central Park

A hot summer night. We're dressed in our finest, our downtown-NYC, age-early-thirties finest. You: jacket, cotton button-down, jeans. Me: plum-colored thrift-shop dress, wrap-around with a flared skirt, violet stockings, and those shoes!, royal blue, bright-bright blue, with heels, my favorites. We walk out of an El Museo del Barrio exhibition opening, between 104th and 105th Streets on Fifth Avenue, stepping into the warm night. There is wine drinking and a crowd behind us, Central Park in front of us, sparse traffic on Fifth. We're expectant, quiet, rolling across Fifth and down the broad sidewalk next to the Park. We head for the Reservoir. Too much to think about whose home we might end up at or even whether we're going to spend the night to-gether. We're not a couple, although we've been friends a long time and this now is a date. Very much a date. It's charged.

We enter the Park below 96th and make it as far as the bush-es below the Reservoir path. My memory is hazy here. I don't remember discussing it much. But somehow we decide we want to fuck under the bushes. Like a dare. Cutting through the what are we to each other. I'm exhilarated. I love sex outdoors. I peel up my dress and take off my pantyhose and shoes. You're fast with your shoes and your jeans. You take a condom out of your wallet. I like the readiness about you. We're surprisingly hidden under the bush. Anyone close by could see us who tried to. But from the sidewalk, no. Not from the Reservoir, either. They'd have to be cutting through the bushes like we did.

We grope and we kiss and we fondle. We finger. Stroke. It doesn't take much. We're each already turned on. And then I'm lying on my back and you're on top. We do it straight up. But the sex, the sex isn't all that. I'm distracted by the twigs, small stones, and dirt on the back of my legs and butt. Your movements, they seem studied to me, like you're dancing. Controlled. Your skin is white and cold. Clammy, even. You come, I don't, you offer to go down on me. But I'm fine with the adventure and want to get my shoes back on. The shoes now are more clear to me in the memory than the sex. That royal blue. I find them, leave the stockings, put the shoes back on. I have a warm glow, but I want to go home now, alone. We share a cab downtown. I love the air.

Flagstaff Reservoir

All water on skin and bright, clear light and Arizona heat.

Ten years earlier. I have a summer job at the Museum of Northern Arizona and am living with other staff on the grounds. I've turned down an underpaid summer internship at the Met for this. The museum grounds, outside Flagstaff, stretch for two-hundred acres on the wild Colorado Plateau. The Flagstaff Reservoir sits on the grounds. We summer staffers are in our twenties, and it doesn't occur to us that our bodies could be unclean. We can't go in alone because the drop off is steep getting in and out of the Reservoir, and we can't leave anyone in alone in case they're too tired to get out. So, naked and swimming, we're together.

Someone has burrowed under one part of the Reservoir fence, and at dusk or later at night we belly through in groups to skinny dip in the Reservoir. Dusk is the best, with enough light out to look up at the mountains, the San Francisco Peaks, while we swim. The water is so clean. The air sharp.

I love to swim here. The release. The full feeling of the skin all over, while letting go of some of the body's encumbrances. The grace of back stroke while looking up at the sky, the ease of breast-stroke. Looking out at the woods and the peaks with the cool water flowing over me.

The Michigan Shore

Skinny dipping with Bruce. We're old and no longer have our youthful arrogance to cover us when we strip our clothes. I have less modesty—and more—than when I was young. Less because this is my body, and I like it, and I feel lucky to be alive. More because I know if we were caught, there could be derision: what are these old people doing naked in the water?

We're living in Holland, MI, I imagine. Still getting back often to Chicago to see friends and do readings. I'm writing up a storm. Bruce is doing his tap. And teaching a tap class for beginners, one that folds in history of tap with blues and swing, racial conflicts and triumphs. We're relieved to like it up here.

It's summer and it's HOT. The beach at Holland State Park is full of tourists. We wait till the evening, and head to a lesser-known beach, the North Ottawa Dunes, on the way north to Grand Haven. There'll be beach patrol, but maybe they'll ignore us old people.

We get there, park, no patrol that we can see. The air is thick but clean. Not much wind. We throw off our shoes, I lay my walking sticks in the sand. We leave our pants. Strip our tops. We walk to the water, wade in. Bruce is happy to let the wavelets wash over his feet and calves, just the massage he needs with his dancing and running. I look around—really, no one. Ah, it feels good to be naked on top. Like when I was a kid and my family lived in the sticks. It was so empty I could run around without a shirt, like my brothers, until I was five.

I'm eager to swim. I dive in. Bruce keeps an eye out. No big undertow here, I don't think. I stay close in any case. Lake Michigan is a sea, a huge one with tides and undercurrents. Near the shore: welcoming water, no fear. Water cooler than the air. Soothing water. And I'm weightless, my breasts bobbing, my legs frog kicking, my arms reaching up and out. The water holds me up, frees my joints. My body. I swim back, he fingers me in the shallows, I come, I suck him. The sex, the cool water, our bodies, the hot night air.

Ladybug

I could write about your ass, made for me, spherical.
I could write about your smooth skin, scent,
voice, your accent with twang,
your laugh, easy and sharp.

It's more than that, you know.
I can exist with you, relaxed.
I'm eating a late-night snack,
you tell me I'm beautiful.
I stay up into the wee hours,
sleep late whenever I can, and
you say I work hard.
I put cocoa powder on my sliced fruit,
getting it everywhere, and
you say do we need to order more.
I stick rhinestones above my brow
with eyelash glue, and
you say you like how the light shines.

Thank you, darlin', with you,
I feel like a ladybug, bringing good luck
just by being here.

Our Li′l Baby Accent

Your early years Pittsburgh, PA, mine Canton, Ohio.
Pronounced *Cáy-in*, broad *a*, mostly silent *t*
You say *thé-er* for there, I say *thayr*.

After ten years together,
is there such a difference between
broad *e* and broad *a*?

Our accents blend. Well,
we say, we've come together,
the two of us.

Created a li'l baby-blend accent.
Thé-er, thayr, Bayby.

Fireflies, Ohio

Zigzagging south through farm hills toward Wooster.
Old barns. Streams. Sparse woods. Crossroad towns. Many churches.
I'm not Christian so those are not for me. The hills are mine, too, though.
My childhood. Deep summer greens set in.
It is so pretty, like a secret.

The sun is easing down. The latest detour angles us west.
We make a drama of this, loving the hills, holding out on dinner,
hanging on to each green turn and each barn. We top a hill.

The valley opens. The sky light dims. The fields are lush with fireflies.
Field after field. The fields keep opening and they are full of multitudes.
We slow. This is wonder. The valley is generous and stretching,
more beautiful than the Grand Canyon under moonlight.
Swimming in layers and reaches of fireflies.
Dayenu.

Seder

Their player piano fastened my gaze:
gefesselten Blick.
My aunt and uncle's,
an antique from their childhoods,
pride of place in their living room
in working order.

With the round metal cylinders,
the same music played the same pressure
on the keys, the same sound.
On another street, on other days,
my Grandma Dorothy
practiced her piano, with passion

in her well-kept living room, the singing
of the keys, the only hairs out of place.
Until her doctor told her she had to stop
what with her high blood pressure.
She was unhappy, but obeyed.
Out her window, her red brick street.

I would stare out at another red brick street,
and at the player piano, when
we went to Aunt Bebe and Uncle Fred's for Seder.

The same prayers, celebrating
our escape from the Land of Egypt.
Opening the door for Elijah, promising

to take care of the stranger, for we
had been strangers, to free the enslaved, for we
had been enslaved.
I was proud
and bored, the service went on too long.
And it was always the same.

I wanted to eat. Still,
the prayers were wonderful, and the songs,
and the rituals, the parsley
dipped in salt water,
the bitter maror,
the songs, Dayenu.

Later, the food, the matzoh ball soup,
my uncle joking with my dad,
his younger brother, them both laughing.
I stayed quiet, watching
my uncle starting the player piano for us
after dinner, my not understanding,

but seeing he was delighted
with the way it kept working,
with the same songs.
I'm still angry with the doctors
who took my grandmother's piano playing
away from her.

Wish I could go back in time
and make them let her be.
But what I miss is that player piano
at my aunt and uncle's house. Its beauty
and lasting. Its plunking music over and over,
my aunt's matzoh ball soup, over and over.

The place set for Elijah, the door open,
Again and again.

May the words, may your touch

with thanks to Psalm 19 and Psalm 45

May the words, the words, the words

of my mouth

my sucking mouth, my licking mouth, my kissing mouth

and the meditations of my heart

my heart for thee, my hands on thee, my tongue on thee

be acceptable in touch and sight

See my words! Feel my lust! Hear my words!

Your words, beyond words, my words.

My rock and my redeemer,

My words, my words, my words.

My love,

all your garments are fragrant

with myrrh and aloes and cassia.

Your skin, your skin, your skin.

Your words, my words, my words.

Your kindling touch.

Mouth

with thanks to Psalms and Song of Solomon

Hungry and thirsty, their soul fainted in them.

I rose up to open to my beloved; and my hands dripped with
    myrrh, and my fingers with sweet smelling myrrh, upon
    the handles of the lock.

I am starving and your scent is all around me; I will eat you,
    consume you.

This this this, is like, and thy breasts like clusters of grapes.

My beloved is mine, and I am his: he feedeth among the lilies.

You eat me and I am beside myself; I leave my body.

I will have you in the dark.

Until the day break, and the shadows flee away, I will get me to
    the mountain of myrrh, and to the hill of frankincense.

Open thy mouth wide, and I will fill it.

Hungry and thirsty, I will devour you.

Until the day break, and the shadows flee away, I will get me to
    the mountain of myrrh, and to the hill of frankincense.

To Fall Back in Love with the Midwest

The Midwest was my first love, the field behind my parents' house
where I could lie, looking at clouds, hidden by the long grass.
No one could see me, but I wasn't too far from home.
The soft prairie grass, the cornfield behind, the creek.

But I got to know the land too well. By the end of each summer,
I was sick of the color green, ready for school to start.
Later, I met the *Jew*-calling, the *Jesus will save you*, the racism.
The price paid for being different, prices plural.

Then I was lucky. Schools and jobs and love pulled me
around—in New York, I saw William Burroughs at a basement party,
dancing with a large, dead fish. Holding it in both his arms.

Next, new love happened, or so I thought, and I moved back.
Not the sticks this time, not Ohio, not fields, but
Chicago, it had everything that I needed. I fell in like.

Not till Covid times, though, did I fall back in love
with the Midwest. I'll skip the whys here—it's poetry,
a place to feel, not an obligation to explain.
I can tell you, though, that even if I won the lottery,
I'd stay here. Generous Chicago, and nearby southwest Michigan,
the coast of Lake Michigan, its sandy beaches.

Here they say hi on the street, and compliment
the polka dots on my down coat. And I can walk
to fresh water, a Lake that's an inland sea.
When climate change and greed make water scarce,
I can fetch, carry, and boil my own water.
Still eat fresh corn on the cob.
And sit on a bench in the park, talking with my neighbors,
figuring together how we're going to survive.

Acknowledgements

I would like to thank the following journals and press-es that first published some of the poems in this collection and their editors for encouraging my work: David Brunson and Ivana Aponte at *Copihue Poetry* for "Hanging Out" and "Ladybug," Mike Phillips at From Beyond Press for "Liquid Psalm to a Great Lake" and "When the What Ifs Turn into Nows," Kellie Scott-Reed at *Roi Fainéant* for the first iteration of "When the What Ifs Turn into Nows," and "Night Walking," and guest editors François Bereaud and Melissa Flores Anderson for "Bodies, Water," Mirjana M. at *Suburban Witchcraft* for "Fireflies, Ohio," Matt Bullen at *Red Ogre Review* for "Clumsy Poem" and "Topology," and M.M. Kaufman at *Rejection Letters* for "Hi, 50th Reunion Yearbook."

Gratitude to places where I had the opportunity to give readings of these and other poems in the collection—and their hosts: in Chicago, Tanya Gentile and the late Flavio Gentile at Printers Row Wine in the South Loop, Zach Cahill at the Gray Center for Art & Inquiry at the University of Chicago, Joy Young and Timothy David Rey at Poetry@The Green, Carrie McGath at City Lit Books, Moises Flores at Umbrella Vintage at Salt Shed, Mark Jeffery at Ohklahomo, Noa Fields at the Poetry Foundation, and in Columbus, Nathan McDowell at Two Dollar Radio Headquarters.

Big thanks for astute editing and wonderful collaboration to the Founding Editor of Tulipwood Books, Lynne Ellis.

Gratitude to Ragdale for the magical residency that allowed me to complete this book. And to Regin Igloria and Ignatius Valentine Aloysius for encouraging my participation.

And warm thanks to those who coaxed and inspired my poems along the way: Bruce Black, Tim Moder, Rachel DeWoskin, Taylor Byas, Dikipka Mukherjee, Faylita Hicks, Calvin Forbes, Thea Goodman, Jenny Lin, Marc Meierkort, Beau Gimblett, Jesse Lee Kercheval, Anne-Marie Oomen, Kate Korroch, Nora Kyger, Bill Foster, Nicky Ni, David Raskin, Carrie McGath, Renee Agatep, Sam Herschel Wein, Preston Danvers, Janel Galnares, Janet Cheung, and more.

I look forward to continuing to learn from you all along the way.

This book is dedicated to the great Great Lakes.

About the Author

A Pushcart Prize and Best of the Net nominee, Maud Lavin has published in *Reckon Review, Copihue Poetry, BRIDGE, Roi Fainéant, The Nation, Harper's Bazaar, Slate,* and other venues. One of her books, Cut With the Kitchen Knife (Yale University Press), was named a New York Times Notable Book. Her other books include Clean New World and Push Comes to Shove, both MIT Press, and three anthologies. Her writing has appeared in Chinese, Japanese, Korean, German, Dutch, Finnish, and Spanish, as well as English. Recently, Cowboy Jamboree Press published her Silences, Ohio, and From Beyond Press her eco-novel Mermaids and Lazy Activists. She is a 4-H alumna and a Guggenheim Fellow.

About the Cover Art

Agila Looking for Land #12
by Lucia Enriquez

The work of Lucia Enriquez includes digital applications emulating particle interactions and wave forms in addition to traditional materials. She draws from Philippine fables and myth, and the landscape of the Pacific Northwest, in a syncretic mix to create images that evoke journeys and the mysteries of nature and dream.

lucidartstudio.com

Publication History

"Bodies, Water" — *Roi Fainéant* (July 10, 2022)

"Clumsy Poem" — *Red Ogre Review* (Issue 10, July 2022)

"Fireflies, Ohio" — *Heimat Review* (Oct. 15, 2022)

"Hanging Out" — *Copihue Poetry* (Fall 2024/Winter 2025)

"Hi, 50th Reunion Yearbook" — *Rejection Letters* (July 11, 2022)]

"Ladybug" — *Copihue Poetry* (Volume 2, 2023)

"Liquid Psalm to a Great Lake" — MERMAIDS AND LAZY ACTIVISTS,
    From Beyond Press (2025)

"Night Walking" — *Roi Fainéant* (March 5, 2023)

"Topology" — *Red Ogre Review* (November 2022)

"When the What Ifs Turn into Nows" — *Roi Fainéant* (June 23,
    2024) and MERMAIDS AND LAZY ACTIVISTS (2025)

Sources

Wikipedia contributors. 2025. "Topology." Wikipedia. May 29, 2025.
https://en.wikipedia.org/wiki/Topology.

A Note on the Typography

On this book's cover, the collection title is set in Transat Text, designed by Greg Shutters at Typetanic Fonts, based in Chicago.

The author's name, poem titles, section titles, and page numbers appear in Minerva Modern, from Chicago-based T26 Digital Type Foundry, established by Carlos Segura.

The body text is set in 12-point Adobe Garamond Pro, based on a typeface first designed and engraved by Claude Garamont in the early 1500s. This typeface was adapted for the digital age by Adobe's principal type designer Robert Slimbach, who was born in Evanston, IL.